THE DILEMMA OF THE
ALCOHOLIC MARRIAGE

THE DILEMMA
OF THE
ALCOHOLIC MARRIAGE

Al-Anon Family Group Headquarters, Inc.

NEW YORK • 1967

The Dilemma of the Alcoholic Marriage
ⓒ, AL-ANON FAMILY GROUP HEADQUARTERS, INC. 1967

P. O. Box 182
Madison Square Station
New York, New York 10010

First Printing March 1967

Second Printing August 1967

Library of Congress Catalog Card No. 67-19832

Approved by
World Service Conference
Al-Anon Family Groups

HV
5275
.A5413

PRINTED IN THE UNITED STATES OF AMERICA
BY CORNWALL PRESS, INC., CORNWALL, N.Y.

CONTENTS

INTRODUCTION

The Al-Anon Family Groups make up a fellowship of men and women whose lives have been, or are being, disturbed by another's compulsive drinking. The members share experience, strength and hope with each other in a continuing effort to achieve serenity. The Al-Anon program is essentially a personal re-orientation process based on The Twelve Steps and The Twelve Traditions of Alcoholics Anonymous.

The groups of Al-Anon meet to discuss the problems created by alcoholism. It is an informal fellowship; its members offer neither advice nor pity. They do, however, offer an empathic atmosphere in which the non-alcoholic comes to recognize his or her own faulty attitudes which may be aggravating the family difficulties.

Al-Anon offers its members a group therapy in which the non-alcoholic, baffled by the problem, can find peace of mind and hope for the future.

THE DILEMMA OF THE
ALCOHOLIC MARRIAGE

CHAPTER I

THE NATURE OF
THE DILEMMA

The wives and husbands of compulsive drinkers often find it difficult to adjust to the personal characteristics, traits and attitudes of the alcoholic, whether sober or still drinking.

This is especially true in the more intimate areas of the marriage relationship: personal communication and sex.

The World Service Office of the Al-Anon Family Groups receives hundreds of letters each year from troubled and bewildered people in all parts of the world. They want to know how to deal with the maladjustments in their marriages, difficulties which often were realized only after the alcoholic had settled into sobriety.

While the active drinking was still the major problem, the spouse wished only that the alcoholic

1

might become sober. That was to be the magic solution to all problems. But sobriety alone often fails to bring about the hoped-for improvement.

The problems which beset the families of alcoholics who are still drinking often bring the spouses to Al-Anon in search of solutions. The difficulties which disrupt normal family life are physical and verbal violence, disturbed children, peril to health and safety, unpaid bills, and often actual deprivation of such necessities as food and clothing.

With such problems Al-Anon has a long record of success. It can and does help those who really want help. Its group work consists of a sharing of experiences; the program guides its members to a better understanding and more willing acceptance of themselves. Al-Anon gives them a fresh point of view from which to approach their difficulties.

This therapy works. This is proved by the many thousands who have found the way to more constructive attitudes toward themselves and their families. They learn to overcome such negative emotions as resentment and self-pity. Ultimately the resulting change often motivates the alcoholic to seek help.

While the drinking is active, and day-to-day problems absorb the attention and energies of the non-alcoholic spouse, the matter of sexual maladjustment often falls into the background. There may be difficulties, of course. Some alcoholics, sexually stimulated by liquor, may make brutally aggressive and sometimes violent assaults, to which their spouses react with fear or disgust. Others become totally incompetent sexually, depriving the normal partner of this vital element of marriage.

The interaction and attitudes established in such ways are often too deep to be changed once the alcoholic becomes sober. Years of compulsive drinking may have brought about radical emotional changes in both partners to the marriage: the alcoholic may be inhibited by guilt over his behavior while he was drinking, the non-alcoholic by remembered violence, deprivations, infidelities and other humiliations. These reactions may persist even long after the drinker has become sober, and both hope to re-establish a normal relationship.

Troubled wives and husbands often take it for granted that their marital discords are due entirely to alcoholism, whether the alcoholic is sober or is still drinking. Yet alcoholism itself rarely creates all these problems, and sobriety itself usually does not cure them.

Many professionals in the fields of human relations believe that alcoholism and sexual maladjustment have a common psychological basis. The alcoholic may, for reasons deeply buried in the subconscious, find normal sexual adjustment difficult.

When a woman marries a man who drinks alcoholically, she may be accepting a sex problem along with the alcoholism. Many a person enters blithely into such a marriage with the romantic notion that love will overcome all—that the magic of togetherness will transform the devoted but alcoholic lover into a sober, responsible husband. This risk is often doomed to failure. She soon learns that even love is no match for the compelling desire for alcohol. And to make matters worse, she may find herself confronted with a sexual inadequacy or indifference that in itself may stand in the way of his achieving sobriety.

In a broad generalization, subject to many variations, the sexual drives of the alcoholic may show two influences:

In the one, due perhaps to early conditioning, there is a subconscious abhorrence of sex which can be overcome only by drinking enough alcohol to break down inhibitions.

In the other, the depressant effects of alcohol inhibit normal sexual desire and the ability to give and achieve satisfaction. This is obviously true when the excessive intake of alcohol renders the drinker physically helpless.

The two elements may sometimes combine into one situation: a man's desire to conform to the image of the masculine male may make him compensate for his inadequacy by exhibiting an excessive interest in sex, especially under the influence of the first few drinks. Following up on this brave attitude, he may create a situation in which he is faced with having to prove his effectiveness as a male. Having taken the aggressive role in bringing a seduction to this point, an inner panic takes over. Instinctively he finds the way out by taking "one more drink"—and another, and another, until alcohol has rendered him incapable of following through on a course which he himself initiated.

When a sequence of this kind takes place in a marriage, the wife's repeated frustrations seem to give her ample reason to blame the sex problem on liquor. This is not necessarily a valid assumption. Such a relationship would obviously need prompt attention from a marriage counselor, preferably a doctor with psychiatric training who is equipped to uncover the reasons for this bewildering behavior in the alcoholic.

Yet one dependable fact emerges: the re-establishment of a satisfactory sex relationship *may* be brought about if both partners are willing to contribute to the partnership the patience, loyalty, respect and honesty which are built into the Al-Anon program.

With this in mind, we have ventured to deal with this broad and tangled subject because we believe that the principles by which Al-Anon members try to live can help to solve this problem, as it does so many others.

An earnest and concentrated study of the Al-Anon program, in depth, will help us to become more tolerant, confident and loving, teaching us to accept the faults of others as we seek to correct shortcomings in ourselves.

Chapter II

AL-ANON IS FOR GUIDANCE— NOT FOR COUNSELING

If we accept the fact that the basic purpose of Al-Anon is to help us, its members, solve our personal problems, we acknowledge that the means we use *can be applied to any life situation.*

What the newcomer must realize is that our fellow members are not equipped, by training or experience, to advise, judge or counsel in specific problems, and particularly not in those involving close family relationships. That is the function of the physician, the clergyman, the social worker or other counselors with a professional background for this work.

For the same reason it is not advisable to look for guidance in pseudo-scientific literature to be found on every paperback bookshelf today. This is very much like treating an undiagnosed illness with a patent medicine instead of consulting a specialist.

Professionals in the field of alcoholism have done a great deal of research into the effects of alcoholism on marriage. Many of their writings include information about specific findings on personal communication. But there is rarely anything to be found that explains how a satisfactory sex relationship may be established or regained.

Such widely-discussed researches as the Kinsey report are no help either; they take the lid off many startling situations but do not indicate a course of action that an individual could successfully apply.

This reticence in the scientist's approach to the sex problem is not due to prudery nor to a lack of subjects for study; case histories are plentiful. It is rather that those who work in the field of marital relations know it is futile and even dangerous to make recommendations. Each situation is unique; each is confused by conflicting emotions and reactions that are never the same in any two cases. The causes may, indeed, go far back into childhood.

Let us consider a typical case in which we can get a glimpse of the role played by early conditioning:

The Story of Donna

Donna M. grew up in a happy, affectionate family. Her view of home life came from a dependable, provident, good-natured father and a warm, loving mother. When Donna anticipated marriage to Donald S., a charming boy she had met at college, she could imagine it only as more of the same sort of life, with herself in the wife and mother role.

Donald was the son of a highly successful, hard-drinking father, and an indifferent mother who used the family's ample means to enjoy life on her own terms. Donald grew up with a succession of nurses and tutors until he was sent away to an expensive prep school at 14. Every material wish was fulfilled from earliest childhood—his parents found it more convenient to indulge him than bother with him. Lack of parental love resulted in character and personality distortion which first showed itself in his drinking at prep school and college. His family wasn't particularly worried when he got into scrapes; they blamed it on the high spirits of youth, and always bailed him out of his trouble, whether it meant transferring him to another college after expulsion, or buying him a new car to replace one he had smashed up.

Donald and Donna fell in love. They had many interests in common and got along beautifully excepting when Donna reproached him with drinking too much. She didn't really blame him; she thought it was due to his having been misled by the kind of fellows he was associated with. Alcohol, as such, had no terrors for her; in her home the occasional cocktail party was fun, and there was usually a glass of wine with dinner.

And so they were married. Don promised Donna faithfully he would limit his drinking. Because he already had secret misgivings about his ability to control it, he resolved to stop drinking entirely after their honeymoon.

The trip to Europe was an ecstatic affair; both enjoyed the shipboard parties, their travels in foreign countries, and the general gaiety, always heightened by a few drinks. As for their sexual adjustment, that was ecstatic, too. This was clearly a marriage that would last.

On their return, Don went eagerly and earnestly to work. He had decided that drinking would be no part of his perfect life with Donna, and she readily agreed. Fired with ambition to make a success that would match his father's, he worked hard, long hours. His work began to absorb all his time and attention. Donna was bewildered at his lack of interest in her, but firmly resolved to accept the situation because she realized the exhausting demands of his work. After all, she reasoned, he was building a career for them.

But as time went on, the situation became strained; Donna was increasingly nervous and tense as his indifference to her continued. Verbally he assured her how much he loved her, and that "everything will be all right soon." But it wasn't all right. Donna began to suspect him of having other interests, and quarrels and accusations widened the rift between them.

One evening, in the midst of a bitter quarrel, Don suddenly put on his hat and coat and left the house. When he came back after midnight, he had evidently been drinking, and Donna was filled with shame and remorse at having "driven him to it."

He reassured her, explained that he thought much of their trouble was due to his tensions. "And so," he told Donna, "I thought a few drinks would relax me. What we ought to do, both of us," he went on, "is to

11

have a couple of cocktails in the evenings. Then we'd both take a rosier view."

Donna agreed to this suggestion, the honeymoon status was resumed, and the rift healed. And both were happy again in the resumption of their sex life.

As Don's drinking again went beyond bounds, his behavior revolted her, and then it was she who resisted his advances, and another crisis was underway.

Again Don tried a difficult, self-imposed sobriety, and again came the tensions created by his aversion to sex when he was sober.

A long course of psychiatric analysis only helped to uncover some of the causes of the situation, but did nothing to cure them. Don ultimately found the sobriety they both wanted—in Alcoholics Anonymous. But after a year, the marriage came to an end.

CHAPTER III

"LET'S NOT TALK ABOUT IT"

In solving the intimate problems of marriage, one of the most difficult obstacles is the unwillingness of one or both partners to sit down to a frank discussion of the matter. This wall between people might be labeled: "Let's not talk about it."

Sex is, for most people, a most difficult topic to talk about. It is so highly charged with emotions of one sort or another—guilt, resentment, bitterness, love—that a reasonable exchange of views and grievances is virtually impossible. A talk may start out calmly, but as soon as one or the other accuses or reproaches, tempers flare, along with the determination to retaliate. Nothing can be accomplished in this way, which may explain why people give up before they start talking things out and dismiss the whole business with: "Let's not talk about it."

Interviews with many Al-Anon members reveal that this happens frequently. The AA member, living his twenty-four hours a day, rightly resists confessing experiences that may have led to the current impasse. The aggrieved partner wants to know how he or she has failed, and what can be done to restore the marriage status.

This bewilderment shows clearly in such statements as these:

"He's improved in so many ways since he became sober in A.A. He's more than thoughtful and considerate. For the first time he's sending me flowers on occasions; he remembers my sizes and brings me fancy little gifts. It's almost like a courtship, but that's as far as it goes. He hasn't even kissed me in ages. When I try to make an approach to him, even a little one like a peck on the cheek or a pat on the head, he draws away and says: "Let's not start anything.

"What am I supposed to think? I'll tell you. Sometimes it seems to me his little attentions are to keep me quiet while he's having an affair with someone else. I sometimes think that something about me repels him. Other times I think he's sorry for me and wants to comfort me because he can't bring himself to any intimacies with me.

"I asked a friend who's a marriage counselor (my

14

husband just wouldn't go with me) what it's all about and she said: 'He's probably deeply troubled by guilt over the way he treated you when he was still drinking. Not knowing him, I can't tell you what to do about the situation, but it might help if you could get him to have a frank talk about it. Don't make any secret of the fact that you're interested in sex and that you want him. Don't be coy about it. You'll have to convince him that you aren't concerned about anything that happened in his drinking past. Explain to him that now you've had a couple of years in Al-Anon and you realize how much you were at fault in the many fights and difficulties that happened while he was drinking. In other words, try to help him overcome his guilt about the past; that may make it possible for him to make a fresh start on the marriage.' "

Another attractive young wife, bewildered by her husband's coldness, tried the age-old trick of being a temptress. She had noticed, at AA meetings, that the women he usually found occasion to chat with were the more obvious glamour types, flaming redheads or blondines, with effective makeup, an aura of perfume and seductively designed clothes.

Since in her own personality she was rather conservative, though always immaculately groomed and charmingly dressed, she limited her first attempt to a new hair style, a slight increase in makeup and brighter clothes colors than usual.

The effect on her husband, once he did notice the change, was one of irritation: "Who are you on the make for, dressed up like that?" Naturally she was hurt, since she couldn't imagine why he liked eye-stopping effects in other women and not in her.

At home she tried other ways to call his attention to the fact that she was a woman, a loving wife who wanted his husbandly attentions and intimacies. She took perfumed bubble baths, donned alluring negligees. That didn't work either. The first attempts were greeted with silence. The final one brought an outburst: "Oh, for Pete's sake, get dressed and let's go out."

What is a woman in this position to do? Her husband refuses to go to a psychiatrist or to a marriage counselor. He will not discuss sex, or the reasons for the absence of it. His wife refuses other outlets. She is in love with her husband and wants no one else, although she has had several opportunities. She feels there is no choice but to accept the difficult continence that has been forced upon her. And like most of those interviewed, her shy attempts to bring the subject up were drowned out with: "Let's not talk about it!"

It never occurred to her that he set her far apart and above the women he found it casually amusing to talk to. She didn't realize that he wanted her exactly as she was, someone to be proud of and to adore. But at a distance! It just couldn't have occurred to her that his inability to make love to her stemmed from his own feeling of unworthiness.

There was another woman who found herself in a similar situation. While her husband was drinking, she often felt such revulsion at his approaches that she flatly refused to have anything to do with him. She knew some of the instances in which this drove him to other beds, and although she was bitter about that, she realized that she had at least a share in making it possible or necessary for him to turn to other women. Then came sobriety, with the customary pink-cloud elation. Although we learn in Al-Anon to be wary in that first period of success, knowing that new difficulties are lying in wait, she was happy for the first time in years. As his health and activity improved, he devoted much time and energy to rebuilding his business. He seemed to delight in being

17

able to provide his family with much better living than when he was drinking. His sole activity outside his business was attending AA meetings and talking with AA friends.

As this happy way of life went on, the wife supposed that resumption of their sex life would follow in due course. But it didn't. He seemed to have adopted a monastic discipline which ruled out all pleasures, even marital. He appeared to be wholly concentrated on developing his own personal perfection as he saw it, in which sex was something to be offered up as a restitution for his past sins.

His wife somehow grasped this motivation and made a realistic appraisal of her own role. Having refused to sleep with him when he was drinking, she did not entirely blame him for his present attitude, whatever its actual cause might be.

She did everything she could to please him, to make him feel he was once more head of the household. Still no change.

As months went by, tensions increased. She carefully examined all the alternatives. She didn't want to give up her husband, but she wanted him to *be* a husband; yet she had no intention of continuing this ascetic life which came with sobriety.

One morning, at breakfast, having come to a decision during a sleepless night, she announced:

"Now, my friend, you and I are going to straighten out this problem of our non-existent sex life."

"Let's not talk about it!" he protested, "it just isn't something you drag out into the open."

"Oh, yes it is. If it's important enough to threaten the unity of this family, we're going to find out what's wrong. I can tell you that I'm not going on this way. I'm a woman, a wife, with normal desires for intimacy with my husband, whom, by the way, I dearly love. I want to know whether it's something about me that makes me unacceptable, or whether something's irking you. If it's sickness—emotional or physical—there are steps to be taken, *if* you want to. But we have to get this thing cleared up. I know it isn't romantic or seductive to put cards on the table like this—but that can come later, when we understand what's wrong."

After a long silence, her husband finally explained that it was his feeling of guilt about his drinking, his neglect of his work and the consequences to his family and, finally, the several casual affairs that involved actual sex relationships with others.

"I just can't get over these things—not right away.

19

But I can tell you that you've made me feel a lot better by letting me know that you really want me, and care about me even though I was such a heel for so long."

This young woman reports that she now knows what honeymoons are like, though she never did before, even the very first!

CHAPTER IV

AN AA MEMBER SPEAKS

As the previous section indicates, the non-alcoholic spouse is confused and bewildered by the sex maladjustment, which is, of course, attributed solely to alcoholism.

Although she may have learned in Al-Anon that no one can understand the motivations of another person, she is baffled by her inability to understand "what's happened to my marriage."

The following explanations, by an alcoholic who has long been sober in AA, is offered only as one man's view of the situation. It may be typical, it may not be. But it does help to throw some light on the attitude of the sobered alcoholic.

*   *   *

"I have talked to many people in AA about marriage problems and what causes them, and what I have to say here is sort of a composite of what I know from my own experience and what I have heard from others.

"The arrested alcoholic's sex problem seems to stem from a conditioning which is so complicated that it is difficult, if not impossible, to explain even the versions which I do know about. I want to emphasize that my conclusions would not apply generally, but only in certain situations.

"I think we might often get a clearer picture of the trouble if we gave more consideration to the original reasons for the marriage, and how the basic personalities of the partners react to one another. For example, one known characteristic of the alcoholic is dependency. He tends to look for a mothering wife, someone he can lean on. When he finds a girl he wants to marry, it is therefore one who has a strongly developed mother instinct, and who, in turn, wants a man to baby and protect.

"It might seem that two such people would actually complement each other and so make an ideal marriage, since each would provide what the other one needs. But a mother-child relationship is, to begin with, an unsound basis for an adult marriage. Apart from the alcoholism, they're already headed for trouble.

22

"Then when the alcoholism accentuates the drinker's dependency, and the burden becomes too much for the wife, she takes refuge in self-pity and resentment.

"Her attitude toward him, unconscious though it may be, is not geared to transforming him into a man of responsibility. His attitude toward her, as his drinking becomes more and more compulsive, is an unconscious disappointment that 'mama' has failed him by expecting him to be grown up.

"When such a man finds sobriety in AA and really takes hold of the Twelve Step program, it is bound to create changes in their marriage relationship that neither one is prepared for. He becomes determined to grow up, to assume his responsibilities, to make his sobriety count in terms of adult living. He wants to overcome his dependency, leave the 'mama' business behind him. But this wish cannot, of itself, change his wife's attitude or behavior, and the rift between them grows wider. They can never return to the early phases of their marriage, for he no longer wants to lean on her.

"Since his wife has been to him, from the beginning, a mother figure, he may also have deeply rooted feelings about his marriage relation with her, and this would tend to make him shy away from her as a marriage partner.

"I am not saying that any of this is clearly realized by the people involved in such a situation, but it is there, and it can operate to change their relationship into something that neither of them finds tolerable.

"Another way of trying to visualize this difficulty is to realize that the alcoholic is basically insecure and therefore seeks a partner who is stronger. Call it a mother figure, a father figure or a god figure, he will, in his mind, build it up to what his need demands and carefully protect this image from anything that might expose its weakness or reduce its importance in his mind.

"I have known many men alcoholics who were so rugged and masculine that no one would ever imagine their being dependent, especially on a woman. They might complain about their wives in superficial ways—'she's a lousy cook, a shiftless housekeeper, does nothing but go to the movies and play cards'—but such complaints are offered only as an excuse for drinking and so are meaningless. They never speak of their wives as being weak, helpless or stupid. This they would never do, because they'd be destroying

24

the bulwark of protection she represents to him, his shield against a menacing world.

"The alcoholic often attributes to his spouse characteristics and attitudes that exist only in his mind. He may place her in a position of super-ego, a kind of deity, and not a gentle and forgiving one, but a punishing one. This, too, meets a desperate need in him. Overcome by his terrible guilt, the alcoholic actually craves punishment because he wants his guilt alleviated. And when she does denounce him, rail at him, fight with him, the "culprit" feels a sense of relief, as though he had paid for his sins. In this way, she plays right into his hands and makes it possible for him to excuse his continued drinking. She, at the same time, has relieved her pent-up feelings about his irresponsibility and neglect, and in this unhealthy interaction, alcoholic marriages often go on year after year with neither one making any effort to break out of this destructive pattern.

"If she is gentle and long-suffering, her image increases his guilt and drives him still further in his search for oblivion through alcohol.

"But in either case, and whether he is drinking or has become sober, he has unwittingly forced her to stay in place on a pedestal where he feels her to be unapproachable. Being alcoholics, we feel like earthy clods who have no right to make love to a person in that exalted position in our lives. In some cases, it's a matter of feeling that we have partaken of the pleasures of the 'devil' and therefore do not feel at ease with an 'angel.'

"Sometimes, because of sordid entanglements that may happen during blackouts, or even through the warped judgment that alcoholic elation brings about, he may equate alcohol and sex as evils, and once he has taken steps to overcome his addiction to alcoholism, he also shies away from sex.

"In other cases, difficulties in making sexual adjustments after sobriety may be due to a too-rigid attitude on the part of the spouse. Let's say a crisis has brought the alcoholic into AA. He begins to correct his character faults, he is learning to take a more realistic view of life. As he struggles to make this slow climb back to sanity, his wife may continue to bring up his past faults. She may resent his dedication to AA that takes him to so many meetings. In other words, he is growing while she is stuck with all the old resentments that keep her angry and confused.

"It seems to me the only hope of ironing out difficulties of this kind is for the spouse to turn to Al-Anon where she can learn to understand her situation more clearly, and how to overcome the faults in her that contributed to the rift in their marriage. Once she discovers that she was not entirely blameless in all that has happened, they can go forward together and establish a relationship of mutual respect, tolerance and affection."

CHAPTER V

A GUIDEPOST TO SOLUTIONS

Some time ago there appeared in the AA Grapevine the first of a series of articles called *Seven Choices for Mature Living*. The author, Robert K. Greenleaf, had been Director of Personnel Research for a large corporation. As part of his work, he had occasion to give a course for executives.

The teaching procedure included having his students make a complete analysis of their jobs and an honest appraisal of their attitudes toward them.

During the first of the three annual sessions, one of his best students, a mature woman executive, did an outstanding analysis of her job and her performance in it. Self-evaluation was the important thing.

When she returned for the second year's session, Mr. Greenleaf heard her remarkable story.

After the first year's class, she had taken an overnight train back to her home. Once settled in the train, she began to study the analysis board on which she had so thoroughly reviewed the facts about herself and her work. She wondered whether a similar analysis of her personal problem—her marriage—might not be helped by an honest dissection of all the factors that made it such a problem.

Twenty-five years of a marriage that was no marriage; each partner engrossed in work; an apartment that was not a home, but merely a place where both lived, and a marriage relationship that was, on the human level, a dismal failure.

"As I sat there looking at my business analysis," she told Mr. Greenleaf, "I wondered if I couldn't apply the same procedure to this problem of mine. I tried it. I sat up all night working on it, and the next morning, I knew what to do about my marriage and I was determined to do it."

She listed and described the attitudes that each partner would need to hold in order to make it a successful marriage. When she had completed the analysis, she received the insight she was searching for. She realized that if a marriage relationship were to change, *the one who first saw the kind of attitudes required* had the obligation to hold these attitudes and behave accordingly.

"This," said Mr. Greenleaf in the article, "is the

root of responsibility, to respond to the obligation which is imposed upon the one who sees the opportunity to instigate a change. Obviously the partner who does not see it cannot respond to the obligation."

The woman who had reached this determination resolved "that I would hold and act upon these attitudes, not knowing, but *trusting* that my husband would respond. Fortunately I had the tenacity to continue this for quite a time without any response from him. But now, finally, after a year, we have a really good marriage."

Reading between the lines we see that this woman shouldered the entire responsibility for correcting whatever was wrong with the marriage. She did not put it on the basis of: "if he does this, I'll do that." She *acted* according to a pattern she had set for herself—she did not *react*. She was totally motivated by a desire to restore to health a relationship that was in serious difficulty, and she did not allow herself to be deflected from her course by anything that happened.

"This," said Mr. Greenleaf in conclusion, "is a success story. It might not have turned out this way. But no matter; it was a character-building, responsible act by the person who performed it. And either way, she is a healthier, saner, more whole person for having acted responsibly."

The interesting thing about this story is that the heroine of it used Al-Anon principles in solving her problem. Al-Anon teaches us to look to ourselves and our own shortcomings. It tells us to stop aggravating our difficulties, and to practice detachment from the problem. The Steps and the Slogans are full of suggestions that would lead us along the same path this woman took with such wisdom and honesty.

Many of us have learned, in Al-Anon, to live with an alcoholic problem in serenity and peace of mind. In the same way we can solve the problems of marriage maladjustments by first taking a long look at ourselves, our behavior, our reactions.

CHAPTER VI

A HELPFUL WORD FROM AN
AL-ANON MEMBER

After my husband became sober in AA, I spent the usual spell on the pink cloud we hear so much about. Although I'd had four years in Al-Anon, my attitude might be summed up this way: "I've won this battle!"

I had read all the literature. I rarely missed a meeting. Then why did it take so long, I wonder, for me to see the light? I have finally realized that I never even accepted Step One! I never released my tight grasp on the idea that my sole purpose was to win the battle with my husband and get him sober.

Nobody could advise the newcomer better than I could. "Let go!" I would tell her. "It isn't your problem. He's sick. You have to get over your own flaws of character and learn to let go."

I assumed, as so many wives do, that being married

to a man put us in charge of him. I felt that he belonged to me and I would somehow make him conform to my way of thinking and living.

I know now that he might have found help much sooner if I had only followed the advice I handed out so freely to others.

So there I was, with a sober husband, triumphant on my pink cloud.

Little by little, I discovered that I had not conquered him. I didn't change my ways. I tried to tell him how many AA meetings to go to; I directed him in a thousand little ways in our daily lives. I resented his resistance, which grew stronger as he devoted himself to the AA program. And the more he resisted, the harder I fought.

Our marriage, as such, had long since foundered on the rock of his alcoholism. I was naturally hoping that we'd get back to a normal way of living now that he was sober. But we didn't. And I couldn't understand why, because I had no real grasp of Al-Anon.

I blamed his coldness on his interest in women in his group; I grew more and more jealous and suspicious. I monitored his telephone calls, went through his pockets, followed him. Finally I became more frantic and emotionally disturbed than I was when he was drinking. Our rows became pitched battles, and after every one I felt greater despair over the situation.

They talk about hitting bottom. I hit mine. I realized that getting him sober in AA was only the beginning; that something had to be done about me, and I had to do it. In my utter desperation, I turned to Al-Anon like a drowning man going down for the third time. Something opened my mind to truths I had never accepted before:

First, that my husband was an individual, a distinctly separate person, a child of God—and not my property.

Second, that my domineering was destroying our relationship, if it had not already been destroyed beyond saving.

Third, that I would approach my problem very simply and leave the result in God's hands, where it had always belonged.

I did it with a single word:

Courtesy.

People with normally good dispositions have no difficulty being courteous to strangers and friends. It is when our strong emotions are involved that we swing to the limits of the pendulum—extremes of demonstrating affection or disapproval. We are so deeply involved that we treat those closest to us as though they were part of us; when they do things that do not please us, we fight them instead of fighting our own shortcomings.

Keeping in mind the one word *courtesy* helped to remind me that my husband is other things beside a husband. He is a man, a person, an individual; he is a man who does a job, earns a living. He is a helping hand to troubled people in AA. He is a person whose life experience is totally different from mine; he is a mind, a soul, a set of emotions—unique in every way. He is a person to be respected, to be considerate of, to treat always with *courtesy*.

From my observation of many marriages, even quite happy ones, there is very little real courtesy, that deference which we owe to every human being, and particularly to those we love. There may be intimacy, togetherness, but what you rarely find is this particular, *unsmothering* attitude of courtesy.

It seems like such a little thing, but it worked for me in changing my whole viewpoint about my husband and our marriage. The thought came to me at the time of my greatest need, when a friend lent me a book by Kahlil Gibran called The Prophet, in which he speaks of marriage in this way:

"Let there be spaces in your togetherness. Love one another, but make not a bond of love. Give one another of your bread, but eat not from the same loaf."

I have learned that courtesy generates courtesy. It makes you more pleased with yourself. It makes others, particularly those near to you, reconsider their own attitudes.

It has worked for me. It will work for you if you have the good-will and patience to try it.

Chapter VII

APPLYING THE TWELVE STEPS
TO MARRIAGE PROBLEMS

Here are some questions to ask yourself about your marriage, suggested by the Twelve Steps of AA and Al-Anon.

STEP ONE

We admitted we were powerless over alcohol, that our lives had become unmanageable.

Have I really accepted the fact that I cannot control another person's drinking? Am I willing to carry this acceptance a step further and admit I am powerless over anyone but myself?

Do I realize that the alcoholic is an individual? That he has habit patterns, characteristics and ways of reacting to daily happenings that are different from mine and from other people's?

Can I believe that these individual qualities were established in him by his heritage, his early training and by all his experiences and contacts throughout his life?

Can't I realize that my trying to change him only brings resistance in the form of hostility or hidden resentment?

Do I want to be responsible for increasing his heavy load of guilt?

If I do realize this, can I justify my criticism and condemnation of him?

Will I try to overcome my resentment because he refuses to be and to do what I want him to?

Will I try to teach myself to stop trying to make him over?

I will remind myself, hour after hour each day, that I am powerless over anyone else, that I can live no life but my own. Changing *myself* for the better is the only way I can find peace and serenity.

I will remind myself that a change in my attitude can smooth out many difficulties, draw us closer together and change our marriage relationship for the better.

STEP TWO

Came to believe that a Power greater than our-selves could restore us to sanity.

Can I admit that many of the things I said and did while my spouse was drinking really were not *sane?*

Am I willing to recognize that the alcoholic situation, with its disappointments, battles, frustrations, money shortages and constant fears did actually affect my sanity?

Can I accept the fact that, with my own human powers, I am not able to handle everything competently and wisely? Or do I still think that I am capable of making right decisions about everything?

Do I imagine that no one else is going through the torments of an alcoholic marriage—lack of security, thoughtfulness, tenderness, admiration and love?

Do I yield to despair because I feel I am trapped in a situation in which I am nothing but a drudge and a crutch?

Then can I "come to believe" that I do need help

39

in straightening out my thinking and developing a rational frame of mind?

If I accept the fact that I need help in being restored to sanity, and that I cannot achieve this without help, I will turn, like a trusting child, to God, Who is always ready to help us when we surrender our stubborn human will to His will and wisdom.

STEP THREE

Made a decision to turn our will and our lives over to the care of God as we understood Him.

Am I ready to make this decision to let go, and let God take a hand in managing my life?

Am I ready to keep hands off situations created by others, no matter what happens?

Or will I still try to intercept each problem and try to handle it myself?

Do I understand that I am turning over to the care of God only my own life and will, only my own problem—nobody else's.

Can I resolve not to "play God" in relation to anyone else, but allow others to work out their own salvation, just as I am trying to work out mine?

Will I guard against the tendency to let my self-will take over again, allowing my old patterns of thought and action to bring confusion and despair back into my daily life?

Will I try to express His will in all my actions and

41

words toward others, and particularly toward the alcoholic whose sufferings I cannot understand or share?

I have done my best and it isn't good enough. Now I know I need the help of a Power greater than my own. I know that help is waiting only for my acceptance, waiting for me to say: "not my will but Thine be done."

Once I have decided to turn my life and my will over to God as I understand Him, I know I must empty my mind and my feelings of fear of what may happen, of the shame and embarrassment over the behavior of others.

In everything I do, I will try to reflect the light and the wisdom that will come to me through my surrender to my Higher Power.

STEP FOUR

Made a searching and fearless moral inventory of ourselves.

Recognizing that I am not entirely without fault in my unhappy situation, I ask myself:

Have I allowed myself to harbor resentment?

Am I a victim of self pity, increasing the agony by magnifying it in my mind?

Do I criticize and condemn?

Do I dedicate myself to the job that is mine—my work, my home, my family, my self-development?

Do I feel compelled to assume responsibilities that belong to another person, to shame him, to show what a martyr I am or because I fear the disapproval of friends and relatives and neighbors?

Do I punish and retaliate for real or imagined hurts?

Do I expose my sick spouse to the contempt of others by discussing his shortcomings?

Do I give in to despair, to a hopeless "what's the use?" attitude?

43

Do I lie to cover up for the alcoholic?

Do I take out my frustrations on my children?

Do I allow my mind to dwell on the alcoholic's shortcomings instead of my own?

Can I learn to keep aware of my dignity and grace which are the birthright of every child of God?

> Day by day I will try to overcome my own faults and mistakes, knowing that this course of thinking, acting and speaking alone can work toward a solution of my problems.

STEP FIVE

Admitted to God, to ourselves and to another human being the exact nature of our wrongs.

Do I see the importance of admitting my faults, privately to God in my meditation and prayer and openly to another person whom I respect and trust to keep my confidences?

Knowing that no one is perfect, shouldn't it be easy for me to concede that I am not perfect either?

Do I realize that the use of this Step will help me to recognize and deal with my own shortcoming?

Isn't this Step essential to improvement, since I know that admitting my shortcomings only to myself would soon leave me open to excusing them and doing nothing constructive about them?

Do I understand the healing relief of honest acknowledgment of faults?

When I concentrate on my personal progress, the difficulties over which I have no control will iron themselves out.

STEP SIX

Were entirely ready to have God remove all these defects of character.

Should I not perceive that character defects are most easily removed by replacing them with healthful, constructive traits and actions?

Should I not realize that God does not *remove* a fault to produce a vacuum, but to make room for one of His ideas: love, kindness, tolerance.

When I find myself thinking critically of "something somebody did" wouldn't I like myself better if I switched off that thought and replaced it with admiration for something nice about that person?

Do I not know in my innermost heart that I could accept the good He has available for me if I were not propelled into resistance by my own self-will?

Do I know that the words "entirely ready" mean my own complete surrender to His will?

Can I fail to realize that such surrender is not a personal weakness, but a strength that will reinforce my courage and confidence?

In the humility of surrender we find ourselves. We become able to see our God-given *good* qualities, too.

All progress must grow from a seed of self-appreciation which is as far removed from conceit and pride as day is from night.

Let me realize too that self-doubt and self-hate are defects of character that hinder my growth.

STEP SEVEN

Humbly asked Him to remove our shortcomings.

Am I really ready to have my shortcomings removed?

Or do I cling to some of my favorite ones, those I feel are justified by circumstances?

Do I know they cannot be removed until I am ready, that while I have any secret reservations, or even unrealized ones, I cannot be ready to be helped toward my goal of a full, serene life?

Have I reached a point of being truly humble?

Is it only my mind that is ready, or do I ardently wish, from my heart, to be taught how to live in the light?

Quiet and meek as the tone of this Step appears, do I recognize it as an instrument of stupendous power to change my life?

How soon will I learn to put it to my use?

Humility is basically a realization of relationship to our Higher Power. In it we accept our human limitations, while we learn about the limitless benefits that come from aligning ourselves with the All-Power which we call God.

STEP EIGHT

Made a list of all persons we had harmed and became willing to make amends to them all.

As I review the injustices I have done to others, do I see a significant pattern that indicated a character flaw I ought to try to correct? A tendency to gossip, to criticize? A habit of taking offense readily and causing dissension? A quick temper that makes words erupt without my thinking of the effect they will have?

Do I see this Step as a statement of my responsibility, a suggestion that I have now become strong enough to make restitution for what I have done to others?

Shouldn't I regard it as an opportunity to make good, to unburden myself of whatever lingering feelings of guilt may still be troubling me?

Am I not eager to hold up my head and say: "I have fulfilled my obligations?"

When willingness to make amends can mean so much to me, to my peace of mind, why do I hesitate?

Let me remind myself: "I am willing to make amends," but more than that, I am willing to learn to be tolerant and generous in my views about other people, and to consider their feelings and weaknesses.

STEP NINE

Made direct amends to such people whenever possible, except when to do so would injure them or others.

How can I make a fresh start unless I acknowledge the actions and words I regret, and make amends for them in the best way I can?

Do I realize what a basic and wholesome therapy it can be for me to clear the slate of guilt for hurt I have done to others?

Shouldn't I start by making amends to those in my immediate family, and especially the alcoholic, for my impatience, reproaches and criticisms which probably rose out of my own hysteria and confusion?

If I have become estranged from friends and relatives, wouldn't *now* be a good time to heal these separations by making friendly overtures *without reserve,* and without any attempt to fix blame for what occurred?

Wouldn't I reap rich rewards in comfort and

peace of mind by humbly acknowledging whatever wrongs I have done, and making up for them in full?

Before I start making amends, I will make sure there is no lingering residue of resentment or self-righteousness left in me. Otherwise my amends will be meaningless.

Let me remember that the reason for making amends is to free my own mind of uneasiness; there is no need to review each matter to see who is at fault.

STEP TEN

Continued to take personal inventory and when we were wrong promptly admitted it.

Do I make a daily review of the things I have said or done that I wish I hadn't?

Do I learn from these daily inventories, so that each day is better for me than the one before?

Do I try to avoid making judgments based only on my own point of view, which may not be entirely correct?

Do I understand that taking *personal* inventory means only *my* inventory, and not that of the alcoholic or anyone else?

Do I always remember to include in my personal inventory the things that are good about me, relishing the thought of a kindness I have done, help I have given to someone? Or generously excusing another's fault?

Daily vigilance will turn out to be a small price to pay for my peace of mind.

Let me take, every day, a quiet time for reflection and review.

STEP ELEVEN

Sought through prayer and meditation to improve our conscious contact with God as we understand Him, praying only for knowledge of His will for us and the power to carry that out.

Can I possibly doubt that prayer and meditation can help me?

Do I pray for things, for advantages, for specific working out of my problems, or simply for the knowledge that the hand of God is guiding me?

Have I discovered that meditation can reveal solutions I hadn't dreamed of, because I have opened my mind to inspiration?

Can I ever say that prayer and meditation do not work because they did not produce the results I expected?

Do I realize that "knowledge of God's will" comes to us only with our perfect surrender?

Have I prayed for the alcoholic's sobriety, meditated on his faults, thus keeping my prayer and meditation on a level at which nothing can change for me?

The spiritual exercise suggested by the Eleventh Step is a powerful force for good in our lives.

Let me not ever think I have no time for it. I would be depriving myself of precious help.

STEP TWELVE

Having had a spiritual awakening as the result of these Steps, we tried to carry this message to others and to practice these principles in all our affairs.

Do I define a spiritual awakening as the realization, within myself, of spiritual values, the awakening of a sense of my relationship to God?

Does it mean to me the growth of understanding of my own destiny, which I alone can fulfill?

Have I expected this awakening to come to me in the form of instant revelation, and was I disappointed that it did not?

Am I willing to build toward it, watching its gradual growth and profiting from it each day?

Having become aware that I have something to give to others, will I carry this light to those in need?

Do I realize that helping others can do even more for me than for them? That "carrying the message" is an obligation I have to myself?

Let me remind myself that in carrying the message, what I do speaks louder than what I say.

Let me not dilute the effectiveness of the help I can give by letting it take the form of giving advice. I know I will never have enough insight into another's life to tell him what it is best to do.

CHECKLISTS
TO REVIEW ONCE IN A WHILE

A. M. Division

1. Do you get breakfast for your husband?
2. Is it a good breakfast for a man about to do a day's work?
3. Do you look human in the morning? "Overnight" hair, makeup remnants, hair curlers, crumpled nightie, housecoat or last week's apron?
4. Do you use breakfast-time to review his misbehavior, or to let him know how overworked you are?
5. Do you want him to look forward to coming home in the evening?
6. If he's in a sour mood, can you keep cheerful inside yourself and not resent it?
7. If he's braced for your verbal assault, can you bear to disappoint him?

8. Do you remind him of chores he failed to do, so they'll nag at his mind all day at work?

9. Wouldn't you rather have him go off to work in a reasonably good frame of mind?

P. M. Division

10. Did you run out to the supermarket or the delicatessen ten minutes before he was due home to scare up something to eat?

11. Was whatever kept you from planning to cook a good dinner important enough to warrant such emergency measures?

12. Do you welcome him when he comes home so he really feels you're glad he's back?

13. Do you ask him about his day, and *listen?*

14. Do you have a barrage of troubles to greet him with—all your frustrations, the children's misbehavior, the neighbors, gossip about who did what to whom?

15. Do you try to make your talk cheerful and lighthearted, even if you have had an awful day?

16. Do you look nice when he comes home, a subtle compliment to him?

17. If he's tired or grumpy, do you stampede him with the plans for the evening—movies, visits, visitors, errands, chores?

18. If he's been drinking, do you sound the war trumpet and start a fight, or whine and weep or sulk? Or do you act as though it didn't make the least difference to you, and try to feel that way inside?

19. If he doesn't come home for dinner, do you sit and worry, or do you remember there's nothing you can do about it and try to make an interesting evening for yourself?

Personal Appearance Division

20. How much did you weigh before you were married? How much now?

21. Do you think you're just as attractive as you were when you were going steady? Could you improve your figure, your complexion, your posture, your hairdo, your clothes?

22. Do your frustrations keep you from:
    a) keeping yourself well-groomed?
    b) getting enough rest?
    c) eating properly?

d) getting exercise and fresh air?

e) finding new ways of looking smart?

23. If you answer No to more than one part of question 22, why?

   a) No time?

   b) Don't care any more?

   c) Want to look like the martyr you feel?

   d) Don't like yourself?

   e) Want to make him feel responsible?

Use-of-Time Division

24. If you answered Yes to question 23a, why?

   a) Too busy visiting neighbors for long chats?

   b) Too much occupied with scrubbing the house? Laundry? Sewing?

   c) Going to work to pay the bills?

25. Did you ever try dividing up your time into manageable segments

   a) for housekeeping, shopping, meal planning, laundry, cooking?

   b) and allow time for the recreation you need: bowling, movies, gardening, entertaining, reading, volunteer work, Al-Anon?

26. If your husband doesn't do a home job he'd

planned to do, or left it half-finished, what do you do?

a) Nag?

b) Leave the ladder and the paint-pot in the middle of the floor?

c) Do it yourself and point our your halo to him?

Children Division

27. Does the care of your children come under the heading of First Things First?

28. Do you minimize the effects of family conflicts by protecting them with your love and concern?

29. Do you take out your frustrations on them?

30. Do you resent it when they seem more attached to the alcoholic than to you, or do you try to figure out why?

31. Can you make a sizable list of the things you do to make them feel loved and secure? Of the things you do, even out of desperation, to alienate and confuse them?

32. Are you too busy to know what they're doing, where they are, who their companions are? To

give them ample time in guidance and instruction? To encourage and supervise their reading?

33. If you have felt driven to take a job, to make up for the lack of sufficient income, have you considered:

    a) the net profit after you have paid someone to take care of them?

    b) the incalculable cost of their being deprived of mothering?

    c) the possibility that your spouse might be relieved at your taking over his responsibility? Or that he might resent your assuming his role as breadwinner?

HOW TO FIND HELP

If you have a problem involving alcoholism, whether with a spouse, a child, a parent or a friend, you will find Al-Anon Family Groups a dependable source of help.

You can get information about meetings by telephoning any number listed under Al-Anon in your telephone book, or from the local number of Alcoholics Anonymous, or by writing:

Al-Anon Family Group Headquarters
Post Office Box 182
Madison Square Station
New York, New York 10010

A list of available literature—inexpensive leaflets and booklets—will be sent to you on request. Our monthly publication, The Al-Anon Family Group Forum, is available by paid subscription.

A FINAL THOUGHT

Our search should not be so much for a *solution* to a problem, or a way out of our difficulty, no matter how pressing. The search must be for inspiration, for *insight,* and one cannot know what he will do with an insight until he gets one. Part of the necessary condition is to set aside one's own problems and needs, even the urgent and painful ones, and be prepared to receive and act upon the new insight. It may seem to have little relevance to our problem or need, but it may, indeed, point to the new way in which our effort must be directed while we continue to bear our old burdens.

ROBERT K. GREENLEAF